DENIAL

pref. p9
see p 80.
93-26

"Any relationship is under the control of the person who cares Least."

Under!

Addicted to need for Love - She doesn't want me - shun sure nbgy (?) worry her. I out of control.

see p 69
p 7/

Yes!

Stop Feeding

The FIRE

Books, Letters,

Toys & at Deeken?

dreaming about

Talking about

her

DENIAL

IS NOT A RIVER IN EGYPT

Written and edited by Sandi Bachom

Designed and illustrated by Don Ross

HAZELDEN

Hazelden
Center City, Minnesota 55012-0176

1-800-328-0094 (Toll Free U.S., Canada, and the Virgin Islands)
http://www.hazelden.org

Library of Congress Cataloging-in-Publication Data
Bachom, Sandi, 1944–
    Denial is not a river in Egypt / written and edited by Sandi
Bachom ; designed and illustrated by Don Ross.
        p. cm.
    ISBN 1-56838-188-3
    1. Alcoholism—Miscellanea. 2. Alcoholism—Quotations, maxims,
etc. 3. Recovering alcoholics—Miscellanea. I.\Title
HV5072.B27 1998
    613.81—dc21   97-49917
                                                         CIP

        04 03 02   10 9 8 7

Epigram

The human race has one
really effective weapon,
and that is laughter.

—Mark Twain

CONTENTS

Acknowledgments

This little book is a miracle of coincidences, those serendipitous moments where God chose to remain anonymous.

First of all, thanks to Larry for his keen insight and guidance—and for being on that street corner the day this book was born.

To dear Don, who after twenty-eight years remains my most talented and hilarious friend.

To Miriam Pollack of Choices Bookstore, who so graciously suggested submitting this book to Hazelden.

To the publishing guru who told me, "Never send an unsolicited manuscript to a publisher," the day after I had done just that.

To the editor who wrote a rejection letter saying, "Recovery books put my teeth on edge."

To Arthur, Mary Ellen, Steve, and Betty, and to all of those whose names I do not know except for the fact that we all share the same last name: Alcoholic.

To Caryn, our guardian angel, who said yes in the first place, who championed this book, and whose graceful clarity, gentle humor, and loving wisdom have skillfully piloted us through these uncharted waters.

But most of all, to my husband, Barry, who reminded me where I had put my laughter, and to my son, Grant, who gives me boundless reasons to use it.

INTRODUCTION

The day I had my last drink, I thought I would never laugh again. Life looked bleak, and the legions of cheery people speaking in platitudes and bumper stickers would smile at me and say, "Put a little gratitude in your attitude." It was too much to bear; my life was over and it had come to this.

Then one day I overheard someone talking about the biggest obstacle an alcoholic has to overcome. "Denial is not a river in Egypt," she quipped. The unexpected pun caught me off guard, and I laughed out loud.

And slowly, laughter crept back into my life. My skepticism gave way to grudging acceptance and, before I knew it, slavish devotion to these one-liners. They helped me learn to listen and to laugh again and, in time, I began to heal.

Learning to see that comedy is tragedy plus time changed my life. I hope the humor herein will have a similar effect on yours. And so, with this book, I pass on the wisdom I have been graced to have absorbed over the years.

YOUR MIND IS LIKE A BAD NEIGHBORHOOD,

YOU SHOULD NEVER GO IN THERE ALONE.

A man falls down a deep ravine.
As he falls, he desperately grabs hold
of a sapling, which breaks his fall.

"If there's anybody up there listening,"
he shouts, "please help me!"

With that, the clouds part and a ray of light hits him. A deep
voice booms out, "Let go, my son, and I will bear you up."

The man thinks for a moment, then asks,
"Anybody else up there?"

ƒEAR

The fear of feeling the pain is
worse than the pain itself.

All fear is about either not getting
what you want or losing what you already have.

FEAR = False Evidence Appearing Real.

Pain is inevitable; suffering is optional.

If you're thinking of committing suicide,
wait five years;
otherwise you will have killed the wrong person.

We all suffer from self-centered fear.

To be afraid
is to have more faith in evil than in good.

It is only when we are relieved of our
fear of the results that we have a choice.

Living in fear is like paying interest
on a loan you don't owe.

Let us love the best in others
and never fear their worst.

Religion is for people who are
afraid they're going to hell.
Spirituality is for people who
have already been there.

Anxiety is fear of oneself.

I have good days and I have great days.
The good days are when everything
goes my way and I don't drink.
The great days are when *nothing*
goes my way and I don't drink.

For every infirmity we suffer,
God has given us a countering strength.

And it shall come to pass;
not, it shall come to stay.

People with fear of commitment have trouble
subscribing to a magazine for more than one year.

Alcoholism is an incurable disease;
loneliness is not.

I may give up hope but never faith.

Fear is the absence of faith.

Things happen.
It's what we do when they happen that's key.

The way I usually let go of something is
by leaving my fingernail marks all over it.

Just remember,
the darkest hour is only sixty minutes long.

Difficulties are God's errands.

It's not the size of the step that matters
but that you take it.

I may have another drink in me,
but I sure don't have another recovery.

Fear exists only when you are running from it.

Always remember,
we are being taken care of.

I can always *act* as if I am not afraid.

It's a physical, mental, and spiritual disease.

There will always be problems,
whether you're drunk or sober.

Being uncomfortable is the dis-ease of the disease.

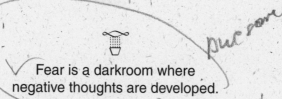

purpose

Fear is a darkroom where
negative thoughts are developed.

Everything is either a step toward
a drink or a step away.

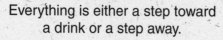

Anybody can die, not everybody can live.

In early sobriety stay away from
people, places, and things.

We are all victims of victims.

cute!

Stay out of your head—there's
no adult supervision in there.

It gets worse,
so you have to get better.

Ships are safe in the harbor.
But ships are not built to stay in the harbor.

Do not be anxious about tomorrow,
for tomorrow will be anxious for itself.

Keep the fear down and the faith up.

Worry doesn't prevent disaster;
it prevents joy.

Face Everything And Recover.

A slip occurs when the desire to drink
is stronger than the desire not to drink.

To dream of the person we would like to be
is to waste the person we are.

AN ALCOHOLIC IS
SOMEONE WHOSE
FEET ARE PLANTED
FIRMLY IN THIN AIR.

A woman goes to a friend's funeral.
After the service, she asks the man's aunt,
"What a shame; how did he die?"

"Cirrhosis," she laments.

"That's terrible! Did he ever try to quit drinking?"

"Oh, no," the aunt replied. "It never got that bad."

DENIAL

Alcoholism is the only disease that
tries to convince you that you don't have it.

Everybody I drank with was an alcoholic,
except for me.

Simply, alcoholics are people whose
lives are better if they don't drink.

The lesson will repeat until it is learned.

When you resist difficulty,
you antagonize it and it will bite you back.

I don't drink anymore. . . .
I don't drink any *less* either.

If you take a drunken horse thief and sober him up,
you have a sober horse thief.

If I woke up today
feeling like I did every day when I drank,
I'd take myself to the emergency room.

Before you pick up a drink, think it through.

If you think you have a drinking problem,
you just might.

I'm feeling better than I think I am.

Live every day as if it were your last—
because someday it *will* be.

Sure I had a drinking problem,
but I looked at it more as a drinking opportunity.

If you don't understand the concept
of a Higher Power, go down to the
ocean and try to hold back the waves.

You can't have a spiritual awakening
until you are in a spiritual place.

Nobody ever thought I was a drunk
until they saw me sober.

The biggest obstacle to a spiritual life
is lack of attention.

If you don't get it, stick around till it gets you.

The harder it is to give something up,
the more you know you should.

Okay, God, you can have my pride,
anger, greed, gluttony, envy, and sloth,
but I think I'll just hold on to lust for a while.

Bring the body and the mind will follow.

The one I always have to watch is me;
I always got myself drunk.

When looking for faults,
use a mirror, not a telescope.

You're the only person who says
you can't do something.

Alcoholism is a disease of denial.

I don't have a drinking problem. . . .
I just can't drink tequila.

When you don't know what to do,
don't do anything.

Alcoholism is my inconsistent reaction
to life on a daily basis.

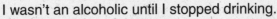

I wasn't an alcoholic until I stopped drinking.

I was an alcoholic when I entered the bar,
and I was just a drunk when I came out.

The farther you're away from your last drink,
the closer you are to your next.

There are no coincidences,
only situations where God chooses
to remain anonymous.

Denial is not just a river in Egypt.

Alcohol is patient;
it will wait forever for us to return to it.

Just because you're not getting what you pray for,
doesn't mean prayers don't work.

You can carry the message,
but not the alcoholic.

If nothing changes, nothing changes.

"No" is a complete sentence.

Alcoholism is not in the bottle—it's in the person.

One drink = one drunk

The bottle is just the symptom.

Ask yourself, What is the alcohol doing *for* me?
and, What is it doing *to* me?

Love

Feelings aren't facts.

You're only as sick as your secrets.

When you have one foot in the past
and one foot in the future,
you're dumping on the present.

20

There are twelve inches between
your head and your heart,
but they're not always connected.

Talk to another alcoholic *before,*
not after,
you have a drink.

The alcoholic is always the last to know.

If I don't change I will drink.
If I don't drink I will change.

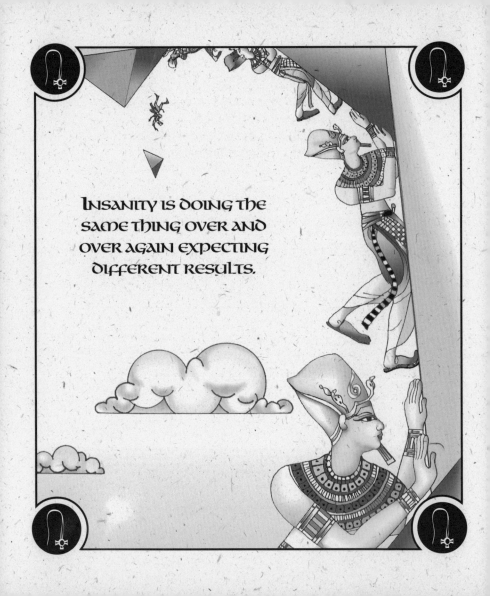

INSANITY IS DOING THE SAME THING OVER AND OVER AGAIN EXPECTING DIFFERENT RESULTS.

*A guy passes a bar and sees a sign in the window:
"All you can drink $10."
He stops in and asks the bartender,
"You mean I can have as much
alcohol as I want for $10?"*

The bartender replied, "Yes, sir."

"Great," says the man, "Then give me $20 worth."

INSANITY

Q: What's the difference between
a drunk and an alcoholic?
A: A drunk will steal your wallet.
An alcoholic will steal your wallet
and help you look for it.

Don't tell me I'm burning the candle at both ends—
tell me where I can get more wax!

Drunkenness is nothing but voluntary madness.

There's no amount of effort alcoholics won't expend to
destroy anything that is good in their lives.

Everything I have in my life right now, I drank to get.

It wasn't my job that caused me to drink,
it was the unwinding from my job.

Alcoholics don't have relationships;
they take hostages.

I must have been drunk when
I promised to stop drinking.

24

When I'm in my head,
I start to believe my own press releases.

There's only one thing worse
to an alcoholic than bad fortune,
and that's good fortune.

I'm not getting into this lifeboat until
I know why the ship is sinking!

To an alcoholic, if one is good,
one in every color is better.

The trouble with being a drunk is that you can never be
sure how many beers you had last night.

Codependency: You're drowning and
somebody else's life flashes in front of your eyes.

The alcoholic's compulsion to have
everything done right this minute is usually
balanced by a rare talent for procrastination.

Sobriety didn't open up the gates of heaven to let me in,
but it sure did open up the gates of hell to let me out.

My sanity is inversely proportional to my expectations.

The worst day in sobriety is better than
the best day when I was drinking.

There's no problem that can't be made worse
by picking up a drink.

To an alcoholic,
instant gratification isn't fast enough.

I need just enough to tide me over
and then I need MORE.

Try to improve the wreckage of the present.

Recovery is a process of
God shaking the truth out of you.

Don't confuse me with the facts.

Humans invented alcohol; God invented the ocean.
Whom do *you* trust?

The things I used to do that don't work anymore
usually cause me pain, either physical or emotional.

Confusion is a very high spiritual place to be.

I like to count my disasters every single day.

Two things alcoholics have in common:
We are all alcoholics,
and we all think we're smarter than everyone else.

An alcoholic will find dust in a gold mine.

I'm a loner who needs people. *Yes!*

Try to remember what the fight was about yesterday.

The paradox of recovery is a sober alcoholic.

Is alcohol the cause of my problems or the result?

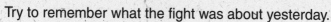

The problem relationship:
excessive demands
coupled with unrealistic expectations.

I drank to get over the effects of drinking.

Alcoholics can be found at the airport
waiting for their ships to come in.

My drug of choice was more.

There are no victims, only volunteers.

I once knew an alcoholic who,
having read about the evils of drink,
gave up reading.

The perfect relationship is when the rock in his head
fits the hole in mine.

An ingrate is someone who bites the hand
that feeds him then complains of indigestion.

If I were as hard on my friends as I am on myself,
they would probably never speak to me again.

Don't drink,
even if your rear falls off or if it begins to twinkle.

Two people in recovery trying to have a relationship
is like two garbage trucks colliding.

It's no wonder your mother pushes your buttons—
she installed them.

One door closes, another door opens,
but it's hell in the hallway.

In the beginning, the alcoholic takes the drink,
the drink takes a drink, then the drink takes the alcoholic.

We can handle the most awful situations,
yet we'll drink over a broken shoelace.

I've known plenty of people who have died
on their way to somebody else's bottom.

It's not the fifth drink that gets you drunk—it's the first.

Don't waste time thinking about what thinking can't
change.

Paradox of the alcoholic:
balancing low self-esteem with grandiosity.

My mind is out to get me.

Those who quarrel with a drunk injure the absent.

Never eat your soup with a fork.

Anything you put before your sobriety you will lose.

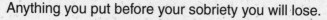

I had millions of excuses to drink,
but not one good reason.

You live, you learn; you drink, you forget.

I'm only a wrist away from a drink today.

Good feelings or bad feelings are the same;
it's the feeling that's uncomfortable.

Alcoholics don't need chaos in their lives;
they demand it.

Instead of saying, "Why is this happening *to* me?"
try asking, "Why is this happening *for* me?"

A woman travels to Tibet in search of the meaning of life. She treks for weeks until she finally comes to a holy man sitting on a peak in the Himalayas. She approaches and with trepidation poses the question, "What is the meaning of life?"

Slowly, the monk speaks, "Life, is a contradiction."

Indignant, the woman replies, "No, it's NOT."

EGO

You can always tell an alcoholic,
but you can't tell him much.

Egotism is the drug that soothes the pain of stupidity.

Humility doesn't mean thinking any less of yourself;
it means thinking of yourself less often.

If I'm listening to myself,
I'm getting really bad advice.

I may not be much but I'm all I ever think about.

If you can't remember your last drink,
you haven't had it yet.

My opinions may have changed,
but not the fact that I am right.

An alcoholic can be counted on
to have an opinion on just about everyone
and everything at all times.

An alcoholic only knows one note on the scale:
Me, Me, Me.

Ego = the sum of all false information about you.

Temper gets you into a problem,
and pride keeps you there.

When you are in it up to your ears,
keep your mouth shut.

Our perception of what's happening
and what's really happening
are two completely different things.

When you are wrong, step forward;
when you are right, step back.

Nothing pays off like restraint of pen and tongue.

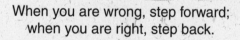

I'm really a very persuasive person;
I can convince myself of anything.

The difference between the winner and
the whiner is the sound of the *I*.

Time is the ego's enemy, not love's.

Self-esteem demands that I make
the least of my unlucky circumstances
and the most of my ability to overcome them.

No matter what predicament I find myself in today,
tomorrow can be different.

I don't have to get emotional about my feelings.

The talents you have are God's gift to you;
what you do with those talents is your gift to God. *Beautiful*

The difference between a demand
and a request is humility.

A closed mouth gathers no foot.

Alcoholics suffer from sick self-preoccupation.

The "ism" of alcoholism stands for "I, Self, Me,"
or "Incredibly Short Memory."

Someone who had thirty years of sobriety had a slip.
Asked what happened, the person replied,
"I started counting the years
and stopped counting the days."

Look for the similarities in people,
not the differences.

Don't insult the alligator
until after you have crossed the river.

I was always a stranger to the truth.

Alcoholics go from no self-esteem to low self-esteem.

Re: God. There is one, and you're *not* it.

Advice is least heeded when most needed.

Humility is that which reduces you to your proper size
without degrading you.

I am grateful I have been given two ears
and only one mouth.

The most sober person today is
the one who got up first this morning.

Your best thinking got you here.

I don't have a problem unless I think I do.

The fastest way to end an argument
is to give up being right.

Examine what is said, not who speaks.

An alcoholic is an egomaniac
with an inferiority complex.

Alcoholics are just like everyone else—
only more so.

Alcoholics' Anthem: "I Was Always on My Mind."

My mind has a mind of its own.

Don't take yourself so damned seriously.

You can't think yourself into right action,
but you can act your way into right thinking.

Reputation is what people think of us.
Character is what God knows about us.

lovely

I'm in trouble when I think I know something.

We are given the lesson of humility
when we least expect it or want it.

yes

Take the cotton out of your ears
and stuff it in your mouth.

Never compare your inside
to somebody else's outside.

If you suffer from low self-esteem,
do estimable things.

If I gain the whole world but lose my soul,
what have I gained?

As an alcoholic, I'd rather talk than listen.

Everything is perception.

Situations don't change so much as my perception.

Try to listen sober—
your ears work better that way.

My imperfections and failures are as much a blessing
from God as my successes and talents.

so when
does my
heal life start.

44

God doesn't make mistakes.

Alcoholics suffer from terminal uniqueness.

If you review your problem closely enough,
you will recognize yourself as part of the problem.

Stop doing what you always did
and start doing what you *never* did.

I'm in pain when I'm in my own will.

Self-centeredness is a casualty of spiritual growth.

Find humility before it finds you.

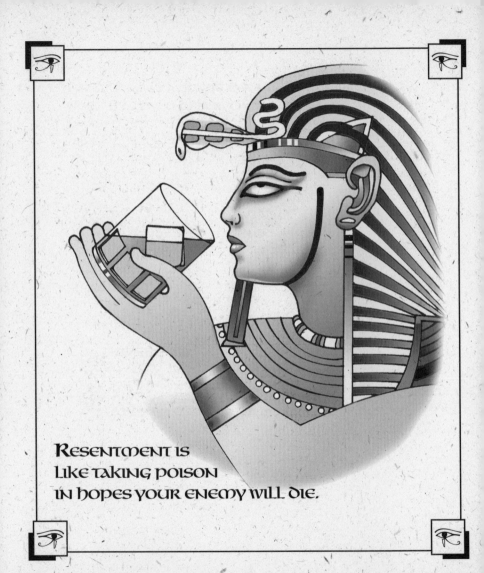

RESENTMENT IS
LIKE TAKING POISON
IN HOPES YOUR ENEMY WILL DIE.

Two prisoners are locked in adjacent cells. One is lucky enough to have his cot next to the only window in the prison. He constantly remarks on the beauty of the day, the changing of the seasons, the exquisite sunsets. For years his less fortunate neighbor has resented his vantage. Every night the bitter neighbor goes to bed, hating the man with the view, counting the days until he will have the cell with the window.

And after many years, his wish comes true.
The inmate with the window is released.
Now he will be able to move into the next cell and possess the object of his obsession. Upon entering his new cell, he rushes to the window then stops abruptly, shocked to see only a solid brick wall.

RESENTMENT

If you treat people badly today,
you get to reap the benefits tomorrow.

Be kind to your enemies—it will drive them crazy.

It's a sure bet my enemies
aren't spending every waking hour
obsessing on how much they hate me.

My old outlook used to be "Look out!"

I like to get a good jump on
worrying about something.

Poor me, poor me, pour me another drink.

When one finger is pointed at someone else,
there are three pointing back at me.

o o o

Expectations are premeditated resentments.

Resentment is like letting someone
live rent-free in your head.

Whoever seeks revenge should build two coffins.

If you're angry, the thing to do is to write it down
and look at it tomorrow.

YES!

Refuse to attack yourself.

If we have a rat in the cellar,
we have a choice:
go down there and feed it or starve it.

Concepts like *slow* and *late* are
always relative to expectations.

We were powerless over alcohol
and our wives had become unmanageable.

Passive aggression:
Your dog is licking your hand
while watering your leg.

Let nothing that others do to you
alter your treatment of them.

The quickest way to end an argument is to say,
"I'm sorry you feel that way.
You may be right."

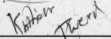

To be wronged is nothing
unless you insist on remembering it.

Resentments are like stray dogs—
if you don't pet them, they will go away.

In order for us to forgive someone else,
we must first forgive ourselves.

The most important part of enlightenment is to
"lighten" up.

Making amends is about cleaning up
your side of the street.

Put aside the idea of fairness or unfairness.

Rejection is God's protection.

Life is a mirror:
That which we hate in ourselves
is what we hate in others.

No pain, no change.

The suggestions are free.
You only have to pay for the ones you don't use.

There is no future in the past.

Your feelings aren't somebody else's fault.

No one is wrong in the eyes of love.
Everyone is doing the best they can.

Happiness isn't getting, but giving.

What fire dies when you feed it?

It's okay to look back at the past—
just don't stare at it.

We never obsess about anything good.

Cynicism is a character defense.

I don't have to attend every argument I'm invited to.

Comparisons are caustic.

Depression is anger turned inward.

A good way to discover your shortcomings
is to observe what annoys you in others.

God may be slow,
but never late.

Self-righteous anger is character assassination.

o o o

There is no such thing as
justifiable anger to an alcoholic.

Alcoholism is a physical allergy
combined with a mental obsession.

Self-loathing will keep you from love every time.

Hate binds you to the thing you hate.

Anyone can hate. It costs to love.

SURRENDER IS RIDING THE IBIS IN THE DIRECTION IT'S GOING.

A woman is standing on the beach with her son when a giant wave picks him up and takes him out to sea. The woman frantically prays, "Dear God, if there is a God, please return my son!"

At this moment, the next wave rolls in and safely deposits her son next to her on the shore. The woman rushes to his side, then turns and yells up at the heavens, "He HAD a hat!"

Acceptance

And the truth shall set you free,
but not till it's finished with you.

When you get to the end of your rope, let go.

You can either let go or be dragged.

Acceptance is transcendence.

Decide to be satisfied with any
results your efforts may bring.

Acceptance is forgiveness.

The good news is,
we don't *have* to drink anymore.

When you accept others, you accept yourself.

If you resist it, it gets worse;
if you accept it, it gets better.

The result was nil until we let go absolutely.

There is a bit of good in the worst of us
and a bit of bad in the best of us.

To the mind that is still, the world surrenders.

Acceptance is about what it IS,
not about what it ISN'T.

Spirituality is not leaving point A to go to point B;
it's leaving point A.

God, thank you for all that comes to me
without my efforts.

Gratitude and acceptance always help,
no matter what the circumstances.

Give time, time.

The record for the longest sobriety is twenty-four hours.

When things are going great, sobriety is good.
When things are going bad, sobriety is better.

The difference between faith and trust:
The guy at the circus going across the high wire
in a wheelbarrow has faith he will get across.
Trust is getting *in* the wheelbarrow.

What if there is no God? Believe anyway.

Don't worry about finding your feelings;
they will find you.

If it's something I want, it's my will.
If it's something that happens to me, it's God's will.

When the horse dies, dismount.

Awesome!
ZARA
3 27.05

The most important amends are
those you need to make to yourself.

There's God's will and there's your will
and there's a space in between.
If you do the work, eventually the space will
disappear and it will be God's will.

If we look closely, we will see we are
given even amounts of blessings and sorrows.

Willingness is the key to acceptance.

If you turn it over without letting go of it,
you'll end up upside down.

Sobriety is not for people who need it—
it's for people who want it.

Life must be lived forwards,
but it can only be understood backwards.

It works if you work it,
so work it—you're worth it.

When you're sick and tired of being sick and tired.

Everything I need is provided,
and everything I want I have to work for.

There are two days a week you should never
worry about—yesterday and tomorrow.

Is this a surrender or a cease fire?

The last moment of your life is the most important—
it is the sum of who you are.

Trying to pray *is* praying.

Surrender means following the
direction God's finger is pointing.

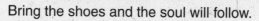

Bring the shoes and the soul will follow.

My life is none of my business.

What people think of you
is none of your business.

Wear life as a loose garment.

Progress not perfection.

We are never given more than we can handle.

Let go and let God.

Everyone must row with the oars they have.

Call on God,
but row away from the rocks.

The best thing you can do is get out of your own way.

Act as if.

Faith is confident expectation.

When I turned my life over to God,
I took it out of the hands of an idiot.

YES

Things aren't necessarily going wrong
just because they're not going my way.

Any measure of comfort requires rigorous honesty.

Happiness is wanting what you have,
not having what you want.

Give God permission.

Happiness is a by-product of doing the right thing.

God hasn't brought us this far just to drop us.

To lose is to learn.

⌐? bargain ?

Don't give up five minutes before the miracle.

Do the next right thing.

You're ready for sobriety
when the alcohol doesn't work anymore.

(prayer)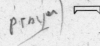

If you want to learn to pray,
sail too far out to sea.

YES

I got sober when I was beaten teachable.

We only learn from the hard lessons—
the easy ones are soon forgotten.

Wisdom is knowing when we cannot be wise.

It's easy to see when things go wrong
but not as easy to see when things go right.

When we forgive, we must forgive completely.

Usury

Sometimes the answer is no.

for me

THE PAIN IS THE ARROW COMING OUT,
NOT THE ARROW GOING IN.

I came.

I came to.

I came to believe.

healing

When the pain is of no more value,
the healing is instantaneous.

yes!

In life, the process is perfect.

Count the lessons learned from failures
as rungs upon the ladder of progress.

A drunk is a sick human being trying to get well,
not a bad one trying to be good.

Material well-being always follows spiritual progress,
never precedes it.

You've had a spiritual awakening when you do, see,
and feel what you couldn't do, see, or feel before.

Recovery isn't a death sentence—
it's a life sentence.

Listening is love in action.

A problem shared is a problem halved.

From Love

All recovery roads lead to the ability to love and be loved.

Well I tried!

Recovery is a daily reprieve
based upon your maintenance of your spiritual self.

Fate is what happens to you
and *destiny* is what you do with it.

There are no shortcuts.

It's hard to see the growth in ourselves;
it's much easier to see it in others.

Recovery is the process of "recovering" who we are.

Watch how you talk to people you don't know;
you may be talking to an angel.

We don't always get what we want,
but we always get what we need.

When the student is ready,
the teacher appears.

God speaks through other people.

The only thing we are uniquely qualified to tell
is our own stories.

The barometer of where I am in my life
is not what I have, but what I can give.

We are sent helpers, friends, and lovers.

It's easy to be loving—
what takes work is to be kind.

Giving is nice,
but giving what I never got myself is even nicer.

When I take one step toward God,
God takes more steps toward me
than there are grains of sand in the world of time.

When you reach bottom, stop digging.

Think of what you did to pursue a drink.
Now pursue *not* drinking with the same fervor.

Live without a sweetheart to love

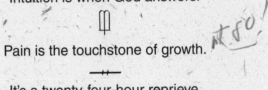

God does for us what we can't do for ourselves.

The only dumb question is the one not asked.

Live in the solution, not the problem.

Prayers are us calling God.
Intuition is when God answers.

Pain is the touchstone of growth. *At 80!*

It's a twenty-four-hour reprieve.

Don't drink, clean house,
and help another alcoholic.

No God, no peace. Know God, know peace.

God looks beyond our faults to see our needs. *then why no Love?*

The shortest prayers are
"Thank you" and "Help."

I have

If you're obsessing about something,
try praying instead.
It's impossible to concentrate on two things at once.

The longer you are sober, the narrower the path.

Mistakes are our teachers.

A Failure of Loving

The things we love tell us what we are.

The greatest gift I can give anyone
is my full attention.

When I feel needy,
I should get up and give.

We are all special cases.

God has no reproach for anything
that God has healed.

Staying sober is simple, but it's not easy.

The more that is revealed,
the more that is required of us.

Sobriety is simple—
it's the people who are complicated.

Always pray for willingness.

I need all the help I can give.

The only way to get to the other side of something
is by going through it.

I have a deep and abiding faith
that comes and goes.

I am Loving EZ

You attract what you are,
not what you want.

The spiritual part of recovery
is like the wet part of the ocean.

Take the action and turn over the results.

Recovery is like trying to drown
and swim at the same time.

A ship on the beach is a lighthouse to the sea.

No one floats into recovery
on the wings of victory.

If you don't know it can't be done,
you can do it.

The past is history,
the future a mystery.
This moment is a gift.

Marriage is the glue that keeps you together
until you fall back in love again.

Expect nothing. Blame no one. Do something.

Experience is what you get
when you were expecting something else.

Live life on life's terms.

It took every drink to get you here.

Limitations are opportunities to open new doors.

An action beats a feeling.

I hear, I forget.
I see, I remember.
I do, I understand.

Your Higher Power makes your life
uncomfortable when it's time for you to change.

Deciding to get sober
is the most important decision you will ever make.

You can start your day over at any time.

There is always grieving in attainment.

God may give you the seeds,
but you have to plant them yourself.

I did!

Do not search for happiness.
Search for right living,
and happiness will be your reward.

I've tried whenever ever it so!

If you spot it, you got it.

While walking down the street one day
I bumped into an old drinking buddy.
I proudly declared,
"Neil, I haven't had a drink in five years."

Neil responded, "Boy, you must be thirsty!"

LAUGHTER

I used to drink in those classy bars,
the kind that had a sign,
"Do not put serving spoon in your mouth."

Alcoholics try to find their way around Earth
with a detailed map of Mars.

Give us ninety days and if you don't want what we have, your misery will be cheerfully refunded.

Having a relationship in recovery is like putting Miracle-Gro on your character defects.

I thought when I stopped drinking that my life was going to be one long dental appointment.

The one good thing about repeating your mistakes is that you know when to cringe.

Now when I wake up in the morning I say, "Good morning, God!" instead of "Good God, it's morning!"

Q: How many alcoholics
does it take to change a light bulb?
A: Change?

If you pray for a Porsche and
God sends you a jackass,
ride it.

Comedy is tragedy plus time.

Some things are so serious
that you can only joke about them.

No one was ever pulled over for
driving while overweight.

Sobriety ruins your drinking.

If you haven't been fired yet,
then you know you haven't been
doing anything very interesting.

If at first you don't succeed,
you're running about average.

There's your plan and there's God's plan—
and yours doesn't matter.

Want to hear God laugh?
Tell God your plans.

I always know the right thing to say—
after the right time to say it has passed.

You always find what you're looking for
in the last place you look.

God wants saints who have been sinners.

While you are asleep,
your disease is doing push-ups.

You can't be fired for on-the-job sobriety.

You're not drunk if you can lie on the floor
without holding on.

Alcoholism is for people who have
an adverse reaction to reality.

Sobriety is the only thing you earn
and pay for at the same time.

On final judgment day,
do you want what you deserve
or do you want a forgiving God?

To an alcoholic,
relationships are like buses—
there'll be another one along any time now.

Sign in Las Vegas:
"You have to be present to win."

We didn't all arrive on the same ship,
but we are all in the same boat.

At five years you get your brains back,
at ten years you learn how to use them,
and at fifteen you realize
you didn't need them in the first place.

*

Pray. God loves to hear the voice of a stranger.

There are enough drunks in the world;
they certainly won't miss me.

Alcohol is a perfect solvent:
It dissolves marriages, families, and careers.

No one was ever arrested for
driving while drinking too much coffee.

If I knew what was going to happen,
somehow I would screw it up.

No speeding in the trudging zone.

A woman was bemoaning that she got sober
before she could taste a Manhattan.
Her friend said,
"Honey, it all tastes the same coming up."

Experience is something you don't get
until *after* you need it.

A Higher Power is someone who makes everything
turn out the way it is supposed to—
whatever *that* is.

Life may not be fair, but God is.

I used to wind up on trains that weren't on my route.

I like the taste of beer and I like the taste of spring water,
but I never lugged a case of spring water home to drink.

When I drank, blacking out was my profession.

Regarding bad things happening to good people:
First of all, things aren't that bad
and you're not as good as you think you are.

I was born an alcoholic.
When I came out of the womb,
I was yearning for the good old days.

Some people move when they see the light;
alcoholics move when they feel the heat.

If you can't expect a miracle,
at least expect a coincidence.

There's a difference between
"I cannot drink for the rest of my life"
and "I can *not* drink for the rest of my life."

My kind of people in recovery
are people from Yale and people from jail.

If I stay sober,
I can always get another job.

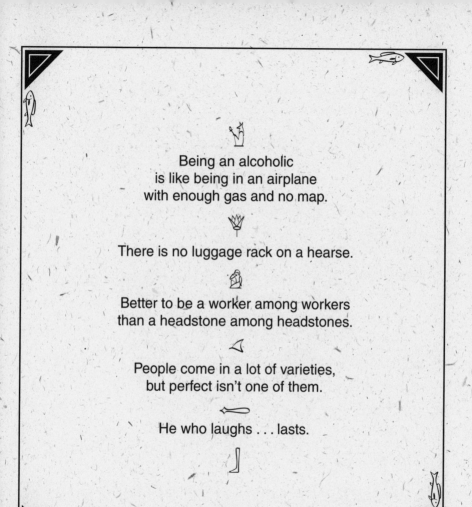

Being an alcoholic
is like being in an airplane
with enough gas and no map.

There is no luggage rack on a hearse.

Better to be a worker among workers
than a headstone among headstones.

People come in a lot of varieties,
but perfect isn't one of them.

He who laughs . . . lasts.

Sandi Bachom has worked for advertising agencies as a television commercial producer for twenty-five years. She is currently living with her husband and son in New York City and has been in recovery for more than ten years.

Don Ross is a graduate of Art Center College in Pasadena. He studied at Northwestern School of Journalism and New York University Film School before beginning a long career in advertising. Ten years ago, Ross left that field to co-author and illustrate a line of children's books. Today he resides in San Francisco and develops sites for the Internet.

HAZELDEN INFORMATION AND EDUCATIONAL SERVICES is a division of the Hazelden Foundation, a not-for-profit organization. Since 1949, Hazelden has been a leader in promoting the dignity and treatment of people afflicted with the disease of chemical dependency.

The mission of the foundation is to improve the quality of life for individuals, families, and communities by providing a national continuum of information, education, and recovery services that are widely accessible; to advance the field through research and training; and to improve our quality and effectiveness through continuous improvement and innovation.

Stemming from that, the mission of this division is to provide quality information and support to people wherever they may be in their personal journey—from education and early intervention, through treatment and recovery, to personal and spiritual growth.

Although our treatment programs do not necessarily use everything Hazelden publishes, our bibliotherapeutic materials support our mission and the Twelve Step philosophy upon which it is based. We encourage your comments and feedback.

The headquarters of the Hazelden Foundation are in Center City, Minnesota. Additional treatment facilities are located in Chicago, Illinois; New York, New York; Plymouth, Minnesota; St. Paul, Minnesota; and West Palm Beach, Florida. At these sites, we provide a continuum of care for men and women of all ages. Our Plymouth facility is designed specifically for youth and families.

For more information on Hazelden, please call **1-800-257-7800**. Or you may access our World Wide Web site on the Internet at **http://www.hazelden.org**.